Stepping Stones

Thoughts Along Life's Path

Second Edition

Rick Hayes

Stellium Books

Copyright 2006 2015 by Rick L. Hayes

ISBN 13: 978-0692578650 (Stellium)

All rights reserved. Published in the United States

All rights reserved. Any reproduction of the book without
the express written consent is prohibited.
The author of this book assumes no responsibility for the
actions of those other then the author himself.

Cover Design by Annette Munnich

Rick Hayes Photograph by Melissa Adams

Manufactured in the United States of America

Second Edition

Table of Contents

Dedication	V
Introduction – The First Step	VII
Stepping Stone – Life Daily	1
Life's Stepping Stones	*3*
A Loved Ones Lesson In Love	*5*
Stumble Forward	*9*
The Little Things That Pass Us By	*13*
Blinded By The Light	*17*
Put Your Coat On	*21*
Inspiration Comes From Within	*25*
A Shopping Cart, A Radio, And A Smile	*29*
A Book's Cover	*33*
The Hill	*37*

Table of Contents

Remembering The Reason For The Weeds	*41*
Sight Without Seeing	*45*
The Family Table	*49*
Stepping Stone – Life and Everlasting Life	55
Created With An Energy Of Love	*57*
Observations From The Airport	*59*
I Can Only Imagine	*63*
Is It Ok To Cry?	*65*
A Pain Without Feeling	*69*
Stepping Back In Time	*73*
Gift From A Child	*77*
Caught On Film	*81*
Caught On Film (part II)	*85*

Table of Contents

Shadows Of Evil	*89*
Do You Have A Reservation?	*93*
A Youthful Spirit	*97*
Stepping Stone – Life Everlasting	101
Why Don't They Call?	*103*
What Is In A Name?	*105*
Feelings From A Cemetery	*109*
Will You Know My Name?	*113*
Ageless Wonders	*117*
Favorite Love With An Everlasting Gift	*119*
The Choice	*123*
Guidance Never Sleeps	*127*
Guidance Never Sleeps (part II)	*131*

Table of Contents

Guidance Never Sleeps (part III)	*135*
Skeptical Learning	*139*
Connecting Through Reincarnation	*143*
The Big Bang Existence	*147*
An Unfinished Masterpiece	*151*
A Lesson From Baby Joey	*155*
Stepping Stone - Small Steps	161
Thoughts from Rick's Journal	

Stepping Stones

A Dedication

A dedication is a place to express your sincere appreciation for those who have been a part of your life's plan. I have been truly blessed, and dedicate this book to the blessings from my creator.

A dedication to the blessing of my parents, for which their guidance and love is a gift.

A dedication to my sisters and brother, for their loving memories continue with my daily life steps.

A dedication to my sis, for your lifelong belief in my abilities. For your belief – in me with love.

A dedication to my children, heavenly gifts from my creator for which the love are blessings from the spirit.

A dedication to life and life-after; spiritual gifts for which I give thanks for each day.

Stepping Stones

Introduction

With each day given along our earthly path in life are the blessings of stepping stones – guidance and protection from loved ones within our given path.

I brought together within the pages of this book a collection of thoughts along my own life's plan. With each chapter I share with you a pondering subject that life contributes in the form of questions or desires.

Stepping Stones is a book that captures my personal thoughts through an ability given. It is a collection of observations along a path for which I am grateful. Stepping Stones is a book that is written for you to meditate deeper into your own life's path, and to possibly observe each step in a different light.

For each chapter's subject, you will find a stepping

stone written at the end of each chapter. Stepping stones are created to assist and to guide along a given path. Solid formations so that you will not sink, stray, nor fall.

Life is truly a gift.

Stepping Stones – Life's Questions

Along one's path of life we enter many questions, while looking ahead for the hope of answers. Questions are a part of learning; and growing.

Within this section of Stepping Stones are questions we often ask, and thoughts to learn and grow toward finding the answers through faith.

Stepping Stones

Life's Stepping Stones

Stepping Stones- Did you know that life is equipped with stepping stones?

I believe that our life on earth is planned the day we are created in our earthly bodies. Unfortunately, along in this plan for each one of us are trials and tribulations. We each are different, and so are our tribulations. Health problems, personal situations, even tragedy, are experiences that we encounter. Fortunately, you have stepping-stones in your plan. As a trial occurs, you take a step of faith forward to learning and earthly growth. You step upon the stone, knowing by faith you will not sink nor fall. We learn from the lesson, overcome our strife, and move forward to the next stone.

Above all, these stepping-stones are held firmly by your prayers to our creator, and the loved-ones who have moved-on....guiding you and with you...
through love.

Stepping Stone – Understand that with each trial in life there is a lesson of learning and a stepping stone of guidance.

Stepping Stones

A Loved-Ones Lesson In Love

A few nights ago my youngest daughter and I were setting in the living room having our father-daughter chat time. Being a young teen, her schedule seems at times busier than mine. When we do have the time to set down and bond, it brings all other apparent priorities on hold.

As we shared our thoughts on different issues, she asked me to bring her up to date on what was going on at LifesGift. Of course, I was more than ready to share the past week with her. She comments that when my eyes 'twinkle' she knows that I have some exciting experiences to share. She has always believed in what I do, herself viewing my abilities first-hand.

As I began to relay to her about the e-mail I had received, the continued growth of the site, and the past few weeks of scheduled consultations, I was given a message to share with her. My daughter and her grandmother were very close, and when her grandmother moved-on several years ago my daughter missed her very much. After her grandmother's memorial, my daughter and I sat down and talked about what it means when our plan on earth is done. I shared with sincerity that we move-on, but are with loved ones to guide them through their own life's plan on earth.

This brought her comfort knowing that 'grandma' was ok, but being very young it was hard to understand.

As I was relaying to my daughter about the past few weeks, I acknowledged her 'grandma's' energy. She wanted me to share with my daughter that she is there for her. I relayed this to my daughter, whereas she replied with *"I always seem to have known that dad, I felt that she was"*.

My daughter brought to me something to share with you. You do not need a 'medium' or a 'psychic' to know that your loved-ones are there for you.

You just know because you feel it.

Stepping Stone – You are created with a gift of knowing. Just listen to what you feel.

Stepping Stones

Stumble Forward

I am sure each one of us has done this at least once. The other morning I climbed out of bed, gathered my senses, and stumbled half asleep downstairs to make coffee. As I came to the bottom of the stairs and turned toward the kitchen, my little toe decided to bang up against the living room coffee table. Sometimes I cannot understand how such a little guy such as the 'pinky toe' can create so much pain. A jolt so powerful that sometimes all you can do is set down and wait for the pain to leave your entire body, which is exactly what I did. While sitting there grimacing and wondering why the morning had to start this way, a thought came to me that brought a smile through the pain.

The foot is like a family. Think about it for a moment.

Here is a part of the body that is a very important, but yet we sometimes take for granted. It is there to help in its own way, to move forward in our lives. Sometimes the foot stumbles; sometimes the foot causes some pain, and sometimes we may unfortunately lose the foot due to a trial or tribulation. The foot contains individual toes, each unique but yet all together working in harmony.

Ok, now think about your family. They are important to your life, and yet at times we take them for granted. Sometimes the family may stumble, even at times causing some pain. There will come a time when we will unfortunately lose a member of the family due to a trial or tribulation, or just from life's plan. Each member of the family is individually unique, but yet the love of the family working together brings harmony.

My little toe is still a little sore, but after thinking about it in a different context I realize that pain is only temporary. Even the 'little toe' member in my family is so very much important to my life.

What about you? Have you stubbed your toe in your family life lately?

Maybe it is time to 'stumble forward' and let them know how much you love them.

Stepping Stone – A family is created with a reason of importance, and it begins with you.

Stepping Stones

The Little Things That Pass us By

Take a moment to think about this for a few minutes. Do you have a daily routine that you take for granted? Little routine situations that you surmise as 'just a part of my day?' I know that each one of us has a few of these.

Driving to work in the morning without noticing the beauty of our earth. A Smile from your children as they give you a hug before they leave for school. The aromas of a freshly baked apple pie as you enter the kitchen, lovingly baked by your loved one. So many 'little things' that have big rewards.

Many times while in a session, loved ones who have moved on will relay messages of validation that may seem 'little' to us here on our earths plan. 'The sled that the brother and sister rode down the hill in front of the house during winter' 'The small gift that mom had received from her son' 'the picture of dad and daughter together', cherished but forgotten by the daughter. These are just a few of the validations that I have relayed during sessions, little things that contained a tremendous value of love.

It seems when we move on, we understand and cherish what our earth's plan brought to us. So much beauty and love, from such 'little things'. So in the morning when you are driving to your job or function, notice the beauty that our creator has given as a 'little gift'. Embrace the 'little' smile of your child so that it feeds your heart when he or she leaves for school. Experience and enjoy your senses from the aroma when you enter the kitchen, and stir a 'little' love for that loved one responsible.

Life is everlasting...and packaged with so many valuable 'little' gifts.

Stepping Stone – Never take for granted what is to become an everlasting memory.

Stepping Stones

Blinded By The Light

As I was driving down the rural road the other day I noticed the large blinding ball of light to my right hovering in the sky. It was a massive circular light, so bright I could not look straight at it for fear of blindness. As I turned onto the interstate on my way out of town, the bright ball was facing me straight ahead. The creation was so bright that even my sunglasses and visor would not hinder nor dim the white light.

As I patiently waited for God's creation called the sun to slowly descend onto the horizon, I started to compare this to another scenario in our lives.

In case you do not know by now, I believe in Life Everlasting, and because of my abilities have had the opportunity to validate this belief with others as well as to myself for many years. It is a blessing that we are each given the ability to determine our own beliefs on earth, in confidence and/or in public.

But sometimes in our life we may have a validation of guidance right at our side. Yes, you may acknowledge that it is there with a brief glance, but just as quickly ignore it. As you make your turn in your life's plan, guidance could just face you straight ahead. But again at times we may ignore, or even try to shield the acknowledgment of white light.

Think about it for a moment. If your earthly plan has made a 'turn' or has changed its course, you may find listening to the guidance of our creator and our loved ones who have moved on will smooth and straighten the road. We may think we know the answers, but actually we are the ones here in our earths plan to *'shield with sunglasses and visors'*.

Stepping Stone – What you think is the right path of decision may be the wrong path for guidance.

Stepping Stones

Put Your Coat On Or You Will Catch Cold

I recently had the opportunity to spend quality time with my parents. Our visits most always include conversations of *"I can remember when you were little and..."* this is followed by smiles, laughter, and sometimes even hugs.

We were setting together in the living room when one of these 'I can remembers' flowed into the family conversation. As the memory unfolded with clarity within our own minds, I started 'seeing' my own 'childhood memory'.

For some unknown reason, I started thinking and visualizing when I was around the age of seven. I woke up that morning to find that school had been cancelled due to an overnight schoolchild's blessing. Outside covering the ground was a pure white blanket of snow. I remember my dad stating that we had around 8 inches of white stuff on the ground, but to a seven year old it was more like eight feet. Although my mother insisted on my need for breakfast, I could not wait to enter the world of a white play land.

I must say that for a young lad, I engulfed my breakfast like an over worked lumberjack. I quickly ran into my room, and proceeded to put on my pants and shirt right over my flannel pajamas. I believe that I even missed a button or two. I found my snow boots buried deep in my closet along with another sweatshirt and darted for the door.

Suddenly, before I could even reach for the front door, my mother stopped me cold in my tracks. *"Young man, where IS your coat?"* she asked with that loving but stern mommy look. I knew I didn't have an answer for the question, my plan of running quickly through the deep pocket of white to keep warm. I can still remember those famous words,

"Put on Your Coat or You Will Catch Cold".
Needless to say, I was bundled up like a fragile-with-care package before I went out into the snow.

Isn't it amazing when we look at our lives how we are 'protected and guided' in some way by ones who love us? In turn as we grow older and expand our own families, we do the same?

I feel that when we move on, we continue to 'protect and guide' our loved ones, just as we did during our earth's plan.

In sessions and in correspondence with others, a "loved one or loved ones" normally will come through to validate and acknowledge. I feel that we shouldn't expect anything less. Our creator gives us the opportunity to love and to enjoy an everlasting life. Think about it, love, protection, and guidance.

"Put Your Coat On Or You Will Catch Cold".

Stepping Stone – We protect and guide through life, and receive protection and guidance throughout life

Stepping Stones

Inspiration Comes From Within

Inspiration can appear in many different forms. Inspiration can be a daily gift of life. When I leave a session, or listen to a friend's words from email, telephone, or on the message board I receive an inspiration. One such session recently added a capital 'I' to the word inspiration.

I met with approximately seven new friends in a session recently. As I was greeted in the lavish home by the guest, I immediately noticed a young lady setting in a wheelchair with a warm smile and a positive gleam in her eye.

The first reaction for many would be a sense of heartfelt sadness for this young lady. She had been in a tragic auto accident less than a few years ago.

Before this stepping stone entered her earth's plan, she is and always will be athletic, popular, and a bright part of the community. With her earthly shell temporarily disabled, her path on earth took a sudden change.

As I went over to introduce myself to this lady, I could sense a presence of positive spirit and a warm embrace for life. I also felt that this was going to be a very special session. She looked at me with a smile and immediately led the group into the living room area.

The session itself was a unique experience (as it always seems to be) for all, but as I drove down the road toward home, I could not help but once again thank my creator for the opportunity to share with others about life's gift. I also made a special comment to my creator for the opportunity to meet so many wonderful new friends that creates absorption of inspiration within my own life's plan.

I had met a person that many would view her life as full of pain, without guidance, and hopeless. Instead this lady travels to schools across the country to speak with young people that life is full of opportunity, while touching many earth's plan. She is not letting her pain dictate her opportunity, truly guided by loved ones, and overflowing with hope.

As our session ended, she asked me a simple question.
"Do you think I will walk again?"
I looked at her and relayed
"Do you think you will walk again?"

Her eyes and her smile told me what her answer was.... she is already walking in her heart.

Inspiration. Appears in many different forms.

Stepping Stone – What we are given within will overcome what we are given without.

Stepping Stones

A Shopping Cart, A Radio, And A Smile

Sometimes we wonder why things seem to happen to good people. The other evening my children and I decided to relax for the evening together with pizza and a movie. As my son put in the DVD, he casually stated with a slight grin *"dad, I have seen this one before. Think you can hold back the tears?"* I smiled and replied *"not if it makes me happy or sad."*

The recently released movie was based on a young man created with a physical and mental shell that was 'blessingly challenged'. As the movie unfolded, we realized that he took the very simplest things in life and embraced them with joy. Each day he would follow the same path, pushing his shopping cart and listening to the tunes on his radio. Although others in the community acknowledged him as one to feel sorry for, to ignore, or to be the brunt of jokes, his smile would radiate as he walked with his shopping cart and listened to his radio. As the movie progressed, a football coach befriended him and became a 'path change' for this young man. Based on a true story, the 'blessingly challenged' young man is now the head football coach at that same high school.

In one scene, the football coach made an informal speech to a gathering of the community. A part of this speech touched me. As he stood before the group he stated, *"You have done so much for this young man. You have embraced him into the community and brought him out of a shell. We should be proud. We should also be honored, as this young man has brought even more to us. He has taught us to appreciate the simple things in life".*

Life is truly amazing. When we look at struggles of

our own, we sometimes tend to forget the struggles of others. What may appear to be a major trial to us, may actually be a simple trial to others. When the movie began, I felt truly sorry for the struggle of this young man. Many would ask *"why would our creator bring a trial to such a sweet energy?"* But then as the movie unfolded, I did not feel sorry for the young man at all. I realized that what we would consider an earthly trial was actually an ability of life's gift. The young man had completely changed the hearts of every person in the community. He taught them to embrace life, to love, and to have faith.

We may not know it, but each one of us have a unique ability.

So push your shopping cart, turn on your radio, and smile as you take your life's path.

Stepping Stone – Even the simple things creates smiles in life.

Stepping Stones

A Book's Cover

Grandparents are the ones we most associate with words of wisdom. Many times I have often commented with the phrase *"Like my grandfather used to say..."* It appears that as we grow older, the words of wisdom become more appropriate.

One phrase I am sure you have included in your wisdom repertoire is

"You can't judge a book by its cover."

In a recent scheduled session, this enlightened statement became a basis of fact.

As I was following my directions to the home where the scheduled session was to take place, I became more aware of the surrounding demographics.

It was as though I had stepped back in time. The hustle and bustle of a city transformed into a serene and tranquil atmosphere. As I continued to travel down the narrow road, rolling hills of trees and tall green grass flowed as far as I could see. The only disruptions to this scene from a landscape painting were houses that infrequently speckled the land. I breathed in tranquility as much as my lungs could hold.

As I turned into the driveway of the home, I observed the neatness of the property. I walked up to the door and there stood the home-owner, waiting to greet me into his home. I paused for just one second, as I could not help to notice the appearance of this new friend. Dressed in a black cut off t-shirt, blue jeans, and a ball cap, the gentleman wore tattoos that completely dressed both arms. With a cigarette in one hand, he asked me to come into his home.

As we sat down, I noticed that he was slightly

apprehensive to my attire as well. I later found out that because of my attire of dress slacks and formal dress shoes, he thought at first I was a preacher. Although on the outside we appeared to be complete opposites, within just a few minutes we began to share thoughts and ideas that were common of each other. I began the session, and the outside appearances of our physical shell became less important. The more we shared thoughts, the more we both understood that the energy within us is what is important. Our creator uniquely and individually created us both, and the differences on the outside could not truly be judged, as the spirit from within is all that matters.

As I reached out to shake my new friend's hand, he smiled and thanked me for the session. He stated that he wasn't sure about this before I arrived. When I walked up to his door, my appearance actually created a pre-judgment of further uncertainty. As I was beginning to acknowledge that I too was slightly guilty of pre-judging, he smiled again and shook my hand once again.

"I do not trust anyone, but for some reason for which I cannot explain I feel I can trust you. I really thank you for this".

I acknowledged that the trust comes from our guidance, and to thank our creator and loved ones who have moved on.

Stepping Stone – Before you judge a book, learn to first read the energy within.

Stepping Stones

The Hill

As I was driving toward home in a quiet suburban neighborhood the other day, I noticed many individuals and families enjoying the beautiful early evening. Many were working together in their yards, children playing tag as they shrilled in high pitch glee, and others walking to bring health to their earthly shell or to create an inner tranquility after a day's workload. I could not help but notice one walker in particular, as it brought to me a thought to share with you.

He was walking slowly up the hill, never missing a step. I noticed his tank-top was soaked in sweat, but yet he did not falter as he continued to climb up the hill. His earthly shell was that of one who included athletics in his daily routine. Yet with this walk he carried a heavier load that created a challenge for him as he continued to climb the hill. He firmly held on to his heavier load, both arms wrapping protectively around what he was carrying.

In his arms apparently was that of his young little daughter. She appeared to be the age of around three, and her head rested comfortably on her daddy's shoulder - both eyes closed. I assumed that daddy and his little girl had also decided to spend quality time together and go hand in hand for a walk as the sun begin to fall from the sky. She had become tired, so daddy had picked her up in his arms and carried her back to their humble home. Even though the hill was a challenge, daddy protected his blessing with love and guidance. He was helping her on her path.

I started to think about how this scenario is much like our loved ones who have moved on. As we continue here on earth in our earthly plan, we are guided and protected by the ones who love us so. We begin each day in our path together, walking hand in hand. Some days we grow weary, and our loved ones are there to pick us up and carry us with protection and guidance.

When we have a hill to climb in our earthly plan, our loved ones carry us and guide us with each step. When the challenges appear to become too much for us and we want to give up; our loved ones help us to reach our humble home as we sleep.

As I arrived home from a long journey, I smiled and whispered thanks. I was tired and had several challenges during this day, but my loved ones and my faith...had carried me safely home today.

Stepping Stone – The hills of trials we sometimes endure are not quite as steep when you are carried with guidance and faith

Stepping Stones

Remembering The Reason
For the Weeds

The life of a person whose plan touched many lives was remembered and watched by those across the world last week. As the media brought memories of his childhood days growing up in a small town to his final completion of his earth's plan, they seem to all agree. Many times they acknowledged his love for family, and his everlasting love for his spouse. They all agreed that his smile was infectious, and the twinkle in his eye brought life into a room.
"He lived a full life" they said, as though he understood life is truly a gift.

As many throughout the world watched as his family shared their temporary goodbyes, a tear was shared by all. This unique spirit at birth was created with an earth's plan. Upon his completion of his path, he must have often wondered if the choices he made were the right ones. He now knows that his creator is very proud, as he did his best with a twinkle in his eye and love for his family.

We each have days that we wonder if our choices were the right ones. I read a sentence recently that said *"We have choices, to plow new ground or let the weeds grow"*. As we continue along our own unique earth's plan, there are times we may feel that our path is becoming invisible due to the many weeds. It is inspiring to know that our creator and our loved ones who have moved on are guiding us by plowing new ground for our path. You may have reached a part of your path that is with trials, but just on the other side of these 'weedy trials' is a clear understanding of comfort and growth.

As I watched last week the story of this man, I could not help but smile. I knew that along his path he too had encountered 'weeds', just as you and I. I feel that he may have simply knelt down along his path and asked for guidance. As he stood up tall with the weeds that he had pulled still in his hands; his eyes twinkled to match the smile. He knew that other weeds were surely ahead along his path, but I feel in some way he knew. This is why he had that twinkle in his eye and a smile within his heart. His loved ones loved him so, and his creator loved him even more, and so he continued with faith.

We should too.

Stepping Stone – a clearer path in life begins with clearing the path in life

Stepping Stones

Sight Without Seeing

The other evening I found myself with some free time to surf the channels of the amazing invention of television. Although it would appear that I would include the 'box of time' in my daily routine due to the fact that a television seems to be in every room of my home, I must admit that I seldom view the small screen. Life simply gives to me a bigger picture that is never cancelled.

With this being said, I stumbled across a special show the other evening that caught my attention. The event was a taped show of a concert, but this concert was unique in that the stars were given a special gift. The special gift of 'sight without seeing'.

As the show began, the three tremendously talented singers were led out by their guitarist to their familiar places on the stage.

Two of the three singers conveniently sat in their respective chairs, while the third stood with confidence behind his microphone.

As the music began, the voices of the three sang in harmony and spirit. As I watched the amazing group bring to the show an aura of joy in life, I felt a tear of happiness cascade down my face. Each of the three men was born without sight. They have never physically seen the color of a rainbow or the face of a newborn. Yet, despite what many would consider a handicap, they are living prove that we are each given a unique plan. The three may be blind in one respect, but each one can see clearly what is given to them in their life's plan. They received their choices given, and utilized this to bring happiness to millions across the world.

As I continued to watch the show, I begin to thank how those still in their earth's plan have a tendency to complain or become depressed about their life. I am not saying that it is wrong to feel 'down' or angry about mishaps or misfortunes, but I feel it is simply incorrect to miss our opportunities given. These three men could have simply given up immediately, not caring about life because they were given 'a trial beyond reason'. They could have been depressed and shouted *"Why Me!"* Instead, they shouted *"Guide me to do what I am to do!"*

Sometimes we are given trials in life that appears to have no reason. We question with a 'why me' or a 'why did they have to move on?'

Maybe the three blind men have the right answer. We are simply not opening our eyes to the music within us.

The beautiful music of your unique plan that is created especially for you.

Stepping Stone – Do not lose sight of what is cherished- life

Stepping Stones

The Family Table

    While setting in my living room the other day I began to reminisce about the memories within my life's path. While the memories became visual frames, my eyes focused toward the dining room. It was as though I was to remember the many joys from a simple piece of furniture – the dining room table.

    I begin to recall the many gifts this table had given to me, and the memories that will never be forgotten. I could visualize my children so very young, laughing and sharing their thoughts while attempting to balance the peas on their fork. The many celebrations as we gathered around the table to blow out the candles or to give thanks for the blessings we have received. I could recall with respect and honor my parents sharing their stories of their own memories, while we finished the last of the apple pie. The image of a personal dinner with my now grown children a few nights before my son was to leave for his career in the military. Each experience so vivid, each memory so fulfilling, all from this crafted wood they call a dining table.

While I continued to visualize each memory with a smile, I begin to think about my loved ones who have moved on. Often I am asked if I feel that those who have moved on will be together and will know one another.

In other words, will they enjoy- The Family Table.

Have you ever thought about why you are within a certain family, whether by birth or adoption? Is there a reason why your father is your dad or your mother is your mom? Why were they a part of your grandparent's path, and why are they your grandparents? It is even a mystery to us why we are connected in our life's plan with those we acknowledge as brothers, sisters, aunts, uncles, and cousins. Why is it that you are connected to your family, and not another?

I truly feel that when we are created we are given a unique path and earthly plan. Along one's path is placed a very special love called family. The family connection assists in our earthly growth from which we learn life's lessons. We learn from the trials that we endure within the family or the joy we experience from the love that only a family can give. You may be a part of a very small family, or a family filled with many. Some may enjoy what appears as a family without hardships, while others may experience a family filled with ongoing trials.

Individually one may hear 'you act just like your grandfather did when he was a boy' or 'you have the exact smile as your grandmother'. One may even find an old photograph of a great-grandmother as a child who 'is a carbon copy of how you looked at the same age'. Whether connected by appearance or personality, each family has a special unique connection through life's generations.

Setting at your family table may be those who were given a life's plan after those who have moved on, such as a young child who never had the opportunity to feel a grandmother's hug. Would the grandmother know this loving grandchild, even though she completed her earthly plan before the child's birth? Why would she not know, she is a part of your Family table.

The family table is one of complete amazement to me, as seated hand-in hand are those family members still in earth's plan – connected with those loved ones who have moved on.

They know one another as they know you, all a
 unique loving part of –
  The Family Table.

Stepping Stone – You have a purpose for the generations that are yet created.

Stepping Stones –
Life and Life-Everlasting

The meaning of life receives many definitions in literature and philosophy. Life is described as a box of chocolates, a bowl of cherries, and a glass of lemonade. We ponder on life after, if it actually exists and how do we accomplish reaching the destination.

Within the following pages of this section are thoughts about significant passages of life and life-after, each chapter touching on selected and pondering definitions.

Stepping Stones

Created With An Energy Of Love

I know the words that I am about to write may touch others in different ways, but I know how it touches my heart.

In the past few weeks I have had the opportunity to be a part of many sessions. A couple of these sessions compelled me to write this article. The subject is the loss of a loving blessing that does not have the opportunity to fulfill an earth's plan. An unfortunate sadness in any words written or verbally shared.

The questions many have asked during my session is *"what happens to this little one?"*

I personally believe that the moment the baby is created and is given a soul by our creator; he or she now has the gift of everlasting life. To me, our bodies as I have mentioned before, are nothing more than an earthly shell. Our spirit and soul has the gift of everlasting opportunity. It doesn't matter if that earthly shell is old and wrinkled, warped with disease, or just a few cells beginning to build, the spirit and soul has already been created. So, it only makes sense to me that I am able to validate a little one during a session. They may to us on earth appear to have been unborn, but are we not given 'the breath of life' the very moment we are given a spirit and soul? Even better yet, our spirit has a greatness of love that we cannot begin to imagine.

Life is a Gift...from the very beginning

Stepping Stone – The energy of spirit is created before the first breath of life is given

Stepping Stones

Observations From the Airport

An airport is a canvas for a masterpiece of people. The other day I was setting in an airport waiting for a delayed flight, and started to observe the creations from God that were inside this building of hustle and bustle. I looked to my left; a young couple was deep in discussion. I surmised they were asking one another if the coffee pot was turned off or the doors were locked back at their home. Over to my right sat a middle-aged businessman. Dressed for success, he was focused on his laptop probably wondering how to land that needed contract for the company. A loving couple of senior citizens slowly walked by, he gently holding her arm with great care. Partners here on earth forever. Then I noticed the area where a plane was to land and all of the people anxiously waiting for the arrival of loved-ones. Each staring into the entrance with anticipation and a smile; excited of each individual's arrival.

Within my belief and ability, I started to think this is the way it is for the arrivals of those who move on. Their loved ones waiting patiently but with excitement, as their loved one whom they have guided while they were on earth prepare to 'cross-over'. Smiles on their faces as they know of Life's Gift. Each with open arms ready to hug them as if to say 'I love you forever, and I do mean forever'. As the loved ones come through the 'entrance' the joy and happiness that will forever be an emotion, as they truly 'see' their loved one waiting for them.

I smiled as I sat waiting for my delayed flight. Oh and yes, the sweet little older lady that came off of the plane to find a greeting from her daughter and son-in-law....standing next to her was an older gentleman.

I felt it was her husband, who had moved on years ago, *guiding her with a smile.*

Stepping Stone – To anticipate with patience, is shared through each one loved.

Stepping Stones

I Can Only Imagine

While driving to yet another inspirational session the other evening, a popular song came on the radio. Normally during this time before a session I spend this time to reflect, ask for guidance, and to listen for direction. This time however, the words from the song became a focus to my thoughts. The singer expressed in the song a wondering of *"what it will be like"," what he will do",* and *'will he be in awe".*

I could not help but to shed a slight tear as I thought about the many loved ones who have 'came through' for their loved ones validations during sessions. How I felt each time they were with their loved ones, full of so much love that words cannot express. The joy and happiness in their spirit unlike us still in our earth's plan cannot ever imagine. Each without pain or sorrow, but full of spiritual guidance and love for the ones that were near and dear to them.

I started to think about the apparent ability that our creator has allowed me to understand; and a gift that I still 'stand in awe'. As I came to a stoplight, I was sure the driver next to me in the other lane was wondering why I was smiling so big with a tear in my eye. But then I thought that *"if he could only imagine"*.

We have a very unique opportunity given to us when we are created. We have the opportunity to cherish and love our earthly plan and to 'be in awe of our blessings each day'. We also have the opportunity of knowing that our loved one's are experiencing what we can only imagine at this time, and guiding us from their unbelievable love.

We can only imagine, and understand the gift.

Stepping Stone – Begin with a positive outlook, continue with a persistent outlook of being blessed.

Stepping Stones

Is It Ok To Cry?

I attended the earthly funeral ceremony yesterday of a friend. His earthly completion to us here in earth would be considered too soon, as he was but forty-four years of age. A sudden completion, needless to say it was a shock to everyone.

As I entered the building and approached his earthly shell, well dressed and a complete vision of tranquility, I noticed the many tears from his loved ones still in their earth's plan. I thanked my creator for my ability, for as I felt to turn toward his dad, his energy was standing right beside him. I smiled in my heart, as I felt that although he felt the sadness of his loved ones, he was relaying the peace and happiness that he now had within. I felt that he was also in awe of the hundreds of the lives that he had touched while still in his own earth's plan.

As I moved to another room, a loved one came to me that knew of my abilities. *"Rick, I can see it in your eyes, he is here isn't he?"* I nodded my head and smiled. *"I know too. Is he sad?"* I relayed that he now has a love and peace within him that he has never felt before.

"Is it ok to cry?"

I feel that sadness is an earthly emotion that we are to experience in order for growth. It is an emotion that actually strengthens the love we have within ourselves. For example, I feel that when we cry the sadness of tears due to a loss of a loved one here on earth's plan; we also experience the many memories that the loved one touched our own life. We cry when we are in pain, and feel even more joy when the pain subsides. We cry when we are depressed, to allow us to remove the sadness and to enjoy the happiness that is to come. We even cry during happiness, as the love within us expands.

So to answer the question, is it ok to feel sadness?

Absolutely so. It is a great emotion given to us by our creator in order for us to understand and to cherish the many beautiful gifts that surround us, and to know that in life everlasting this gift on earth will be left behind...on earth.

Later on, as I we laid his earthly shell into the earth I looked down beside me. There next to me on the ground was a shiny new penny, heads up. I smiled, as I knew this was a physical message to let me know that he was 'anew' and for his loved ones to keep their 'heads up in happiness, as he was'. I approached the friend and put it in her hand. *"I just found this beside me on the ground".* She looked at me, and I could tell immediately that she knew also. As one small tear fell from her eye, she smiled with faith.

Stepping Stone – Sadness is a true emotion given for a reason, to expand the happiness that is yet to come.

Stepping Stones

A Pain Without Feeling

In today's earthly society, man has advanced in wisdom and knowledge. This is especially true in the field of health and medicine. Forty years ago when one had a mild heart attack, medical professionals were limited to their solutions. Fifty years ago when the horrific disease of cancer struck a family member, comfort was all that could be done. Even a slight case of a cold seventy years ago could mean the end of an earthly plan.

Today, the advancements of medicine are astounding and man continues to ask for guidance as to bring an end for many earthly diseases.

Unfortunately, the pain within a physical shell remains during circumstances that are beyond control. Watching a loved one endure physical pain during a disease is dire emotional pain for his/her family and friends.

Hope among all slowly slips away, like the trickle of a tear that cascades down the face of that loved one. We want the disease to go away, and for our loved one to be released from the pain.

Would it be great to know that they are?

In many sessions, the question is asked *"Did he/she feel the pain?"*

I feel that the pain of the physical shell is just that, the pain of the physical shell. As you know, I feel that each of us is a unique and individual energy (spirit) that lives within a physical shell. We each have an earthly plan, but each plan is once again an individual and unique path. When the path includes a 'sudden completion', this may include a deterioration of the physical shell. As the paths completion becomes nearer to end, the energy (spirit) is 'separated' from the physical shell. For example, have you ever had a foot 'go to sleep' on you? For several minutes it is completely numb. You know it is there as you can see it, but when you touch the foot you cannot feel it. Eventually you stand up and try to bring the 'life' back into the foot.

Pain is an earthly emotion that is not a part of when we move on. When our earthly shell (body) becomes full of pain at the end of the plan, our energy (spirit) begins life everlasting and the pain is no longer available. It is replaced with love, happiness, and faith.

Our medical advancements have and will continue to amaze as we continue, but our creator has given to us a great gift that eliminates pain. The opportunity to live life each and every day...
and on toward everlasting.

Stepping Stone – Pain experienced within our physical shell is left behind – with our physical shell

Stepping Stones

Stepping Back In Time

   Opening the door to the two-story building transmitted a sense of walking back in time. I had received a request for a Session recently, and was to meet at the owner's place of business. I later found the reason was due to the odd occurrences within the historical structure. Located in the heart of a friendly town that is rich in history, the interior of the brick structure included beautiful hardwood floors; plaster walls, decorative tin ceiling, and dark wood crown molding.

   As I walked toward the group, I immediately acknowledged the presence of a man and a woman. He was wearing a 'baker's apron' and stood behind the old wood counter as if waiting for my order. She was standing nearby, in a dress of the early 1900's. I felt a sense of respect from the couple, as I set down with the Session group.

As I began, I acknowledged the couple to the group. The owner quickly responded by stating the original owners were a couple that ran a small candy store within. She also stated this was one of the reasons why I was asked to attend, as she and her fellow employees had experienced many strange occurrences since opening the business. This included hearing someone walking across the main area at night, cabinet doors opening and shutting, and lights turning on and off without any sense of reason. The couple behind the counter smiled, and I knew they were simply relaying a 'physical validation'.

The owner asked me a question I have been asked several times.

"Why do those who are not connected to me remain in this building?"

As I have written in my book "You're Not Crazy, You Have A Ghost", a house (or a building in this case) is built with love and filled with memories of those who made the house a home. Each one of us has a memory that fills us with happiness.

This may be as a child where we had our own room and a backyard that seemed to have gone forever. It may have been a first home that was purchased for the family, and shared within the home many years of memories. alternatively, as in this case, a business that was built with love and dedication from the heart.

When one moves on, they have a 'choice' to guide and protect those that are still in earth's plan. They may have been a stranger to you, but being a part of their memory (as living within the home or the owner of a business) – you become a part of their family.

Physical validations are simply to acknowledge their presence. Things that go 'bump in the night' are not to address your fears, but rather to relay a message.
The message of respect and guidance.

Stepping Stone – What may be a structure for some, are eternal memories for others.

Stepping Stones

Gift From A Child

Words from a child are at times more valuable then any scientist or lecturer can ever establish.

While attending service of a dear friend whose earthly plan completed with tremendous gifts, his daughter shared with us the valuable words from her own three year old daughter regarding her grandfather. As tears flowed down her face, she looked out into the congregation and told of receiving the heartbreaking phone call that dad had passed. Although he had been battling the deterioration of his earthly shell for several months, he remained strong for the family. She then shared that as she wept in loving sadness, her young daughter said something that brought her comfort. With the eyes of an angel and the tiny voice of faith, the little one looked at her and said

"Mommy, grandpa is happy and ok now."

The amazing beauty within the interior walls of the church seemed to me as being overshadowed by these simple but amazing words from a child. Even as the priest voiced the scriptures of faith and comfort from our loving creator, I felt as though the words from an innocent child continued to remain as an example of the gifts we are given. I looked down the empty pew from where I sat and smiled, as I too felt the same.

Children appear to be very perceptive to life's energies, and I feel as it is due to the pure spirit that we are all created with. Each one of us is unique upon creation, with a spirit within created to enjoy life and life-everlasting. Our creator has so much love for us that we are each also given a unique earthly shell (or body) for which we are to continue along our earthly path. A child is created with characteristics (physically and psychologically) of the parents, as though to remind us of the beauty of family and the importance of the love from a family. Our energy (or spirit) is although, unique like no other.

When created, this energy is pure of thought and perception. As a newborn creation, we are uncorrupted by the earthly thoughts and description. We are able to perceive the energy and spirit, undaunted by the world around us. Remember the 'imaginary friend' you had or your child may have? Or how our young children appear to have 'heard or seen' someone that supposedly has moved on? As one grows older, I feel that society gives to us lessons to 'block' this perception. We are told as a child that what we see or hear is 'imagination and coincidence' or to 'just ignore, it is not real' and therefore begin to block the ability to perceive. We each have the ability to perceive, but we tend to 'block' this ability that is within us.

As an adult, can you recall having a 'gut-feeling' not to do something? If you are female, have you ever had 'women's intuition'? I feel that during these moments we are simply utilizing the gift that we are given when created.

As I left the beauty and serenity of the church, I knew that my friend had heard the words spoken. I also felt that as his daughter shared with us the words from his granddaughter, he was standing there next to her smiling and nodding his head.

His granddaughter knew *he was happy and ok, and with his loved ones forever.*

Stepping Stone – One is never too old or too young to learn – and to Listen

Stepping Stones

Caught On Film

A picture is worth a thousand words.
A quote many have heard and to some degree a true statement. A conclusion has been established that what we view will remain in memory longer than what we hear. For example, can you recall in memory a very happy experience when you were young?

I can vividly recall being at the age of six and experiencing Christmas morning. I can still see the darkness of the early morn as I sneaked into the living room while my parents were sound asleep. In my mind is the silhouette of the large tree, and placed underneath the shape of the packages that were to be unwrapped hours later. I can still see that one special present that I was hoping for, placed just to the right of all the other packages. To this day I can still remember walking down the hall back to my room and waiting impatiently for the sun to brighten the morning to wake the others.

What I cannot recall is the words that were spoken during the morning, but I can see the smiles. I am sure there were 'wows!' and 'thank you, this is just what I wanted!' Our mind maintains memories similar to a photograph; it captures in detail the memory of yesterday.

So the question is can a spirit be captured on film (pictures, video, etc.) and in addition is it bad luck to keep a photo of the loved one (when they move on) in your residence?

The latter part of the question is based on the presumption that the photograph has captured 'a part of the spirit'. In my book *"You're Not Crazy, You Have A Ghost"* I share my thoughts on what I define as 'physical validations' or in this article 'photographs of spirits'. I feel that 'physical validations' are simply 'tools of evidence' to validate our loved-ones presence.

They utilize the opportunity to say 'yes we are with you' and to relay messages.

For example; if you were the guest-of honor at a dinner party would you enter through the front door so everyone would know you have arrived or would you remain inconspicuous and silently enter through the back door and hide in a corner? Of course you would enter through the front door so that all would know you are at the dinner party.

The same for our loved ones who have moved on and captured on film. Do you feel when they are caught on film they say 'oops I am caught!'? Our loved-ones are simply utilizing a perfect time to relay 'A validation for you to know that I am with you'. I am sure you have several photographs without any 'spiritual evidence' and have asked why in some photographs and not in others. Review the photographs that include the physical validation. Ask the questions 'Who, What, Why, Where, and Time'. Again I feel they are simply validating their presence and to relay a message.

It is not intended to frighten us when we capture the loved one who has moved on in a photograph, *it is intended for us to 'Listen'.*

Stepping Stone – A validation of presence is an acknowledgement of guidance.

Stepping Stones

Caught On Film (part II)

In the last chapter I shared with you my thoughts regarding energies appearing in photographs. Recently I received a very interesting question regarding capturing a part of the spirit within the photograph. Passed down from generation to generation was the thought that a photograph of one who has moved on will not only bring negative vibes into the home, but will not allow this spirit to rest. Added to this belief was the each time you snap a picture, this in a sense also 'takes' a 'piece of your spirit', whereby when one moves on a part of this energy remains within the photograph. Some have defined this also as 'leaving an imprint' of the spirit, similar I conclude as a fingerprint or in a physical sense DNA.

Spend a moment looking into a mirror. What do you see in this reflection of your physical self? Does the reflection appears different then yesterday? How about one year ago? So even if the reflection that you are viewing is different then before, are you not you? Do you feel within that a part of you is missing from the last time you looked into a mirror? Not really, you are still you.

I feel a photograph is the same analysis. It is a reflection of that moment, and a memory for us to reflect upon. The spirit when created is a unique and complete energy. Although our physical shell (body) may age or lose a part due to misfortune, our spiritual energy remains whole. A photograph is simply a memory for us to remember our loved ones within their earthly shell.

In Sessions/TeleSessions a loved one who has moved on will relay a message to 'view the photograph' to their loved ones still in earth's plan. I do not feel they are relaying that a part of their spirit is within this photograph, but rather a loving memory of certain time or thought.

The photograph is imprinted with the memory, of a love that always remains.

Stepping Stone – Memories are captured within – the spirit captures the love to share eternally.

Stepping Stones

Shadows Of Evil

"What evil the darkness brings" – a line from a movie that often is a question brought to my attention.

In a recent radio interview I was asked if I have ever encountered 'evil spirits' and if ever been harmed by such. The answer to the question was interpreted with sincerity and fact on a personal point of view.

As a teenager in a small town, driving to a larger city and 'seeing a movie' was a part of our routine. One Friday evening several of my friends and I decided to go see a movie that 'everyone was talking about'. We were told that the end of the movie will bring chills, screams, and nightmares. The movie's subject was based on an 'evil spirit' that brought harm and death to those that it encountered. We decided that we were 'man' enough to see the movie, even joking that only wimps would scream.

I will never forget that evening. The four 'men' setting in their theatre seats were frightened to the point of actually almost hugging each other. We jumped, screamed, and forgot that we were the 'men' that we thought we were. On the drive back to our small town, we shared our thoughts in shaky voice tones. The darkness along the eerie road illuminated only by the headlights, and the shadow of the trees became spirits of evil within our minds.

Arriving at one of the parent's homes, we spent the rest of the night wide awake together in the living room. Somehow, the movie had brought harm to these four teenage men. By creating a thought of evil through the sights and sounds of the cinema, we were too frightened to return to our normal routine. The spirit of evil thought had truly succeeded.

The definition of evil is *an arising from bad character or conduct. To cause discomfort or repulsion. Something that brings sorrow, distress, or calamity.* The earthly character may be experienced in one's earthly plan based on choice, or one could even possess this character within based on choice. The point is that evil is a character that is of the earth's plan. I feel that when one moves on, the character that is formed in earth's plan remains in earth's plan. This character is not a part of our creator's plan and therefore is not 'carried over'.

So what about the strange and frightening instances that has been validated as evil and harm? Again I am not one to state for a fact that 'evil spirits' may possibly be acknowledged, but I feel our thoughts assist in these acknowledgements. As in the experience of the four young men, their thoughts created additional discomfort, distress, and calamity. Could the 'evil spirit' be attempting to bring you physical harm, or simply trying to get your attention to relay a message. In my book (*You're Not Crazy, You Have A Ghost*); I share my personal thoughts that by validating through Listening, we often find that the shadows of the trees that become spirits of evil are expanded through our earthly thoughts.

By learning to Listen, we soon find that it is once again a spirit of guidance and the character of evil is left where it was created; on earth.

Stepping Stone – The spirit of evil is created on earth – and remains on earth

Stepping Stones

Do You Have A Reservation?

There is something about an old black and white movie.

When I have the opportunity to find my comfort zone on the sofa with a bowl of fresh popcorn, I will search for a film created from years ago. I do enjoy new feature films, but there is just something about a film's aura of yesteryear.

One recent evening I had such an opportunity, and came across a movie that became a thread of thought for this article. Filmed in the early fifties, the movie was based at an exquisite seaside hotel. The first few minutes allowed the viewer to know the movie was based on a melodramatic plot, complete with a twist.

As I reached into the bag of popped kernels enjoying the twists and turns of the film, I found what really intrigued me was the backdrop of the film, the exquisite seaside hotel.

One would enter the hotel through the polished brass revolving door, into a lobby that appeared to never end in size. The marble floor appeared to gleam in sunlight with each step, and the front desk rich in the warmth of mahogany. The lush carpet that sent greetings as one would leave the elevator from each floor's hallway. You could feel the hospitality from the hotel employees as they greeted each guest as if of royalty. The movie may have been filmed without today's color effects, but the viewer had his own paintbrush.

Often I am asked if I ever receive messages while visiting old historic places such as the seaside hotel of yesteryear, and if so why would loved ones remain in places such as these.

Can you recall a favorite vacation with family or a loved one taken many years ago? It may have been at a seaside hotel as described in this article. Along with the probability that you may recall the decorum, the laughter and happiness with your loved ones is within your paintbrush of memory.

What if you returned many years later to the hotel only to find the structure to be taken over with the decay of time? Would this eliminate your beautiful memories from the past, or would you stand in the lobby and recall the happiness from another time in your earthly plan?

I feel when a loved one moves on; the memories of happiness and joy remain. A paintbrush for guiding those loved ones still in their earth's plan. What may look like a structure of decay to us, are the memories of gleaming marble and warm mahogany to those who have moved on. The reservations within these structures include check-in and check-out times for those who have moved on. They check in to guide you upon your visit, and check out when they have relayed the messages of memories to those that visit.

As I finished the last kernel of popcorn, I wondered if

those in the black and white movie are now enjoying the beautiful color of guiding those who visit this seaside hotel today.

Maybe if I visit, they will share a message.

Stepping Stone – Spiritual energies are tour guides for understanding lessons learned

Stepping Stones

A Youthful Spirit

Act now and we will send you an additional 30 day supply of 'Wrinkles Away', and look twenty years younger!

Turn on a television or radio, flip through the magazine ads or the internet spam email and you will hear all of the 'new younger look' products available in today's market. Even the specialists in the surgical field have presented options for us to look younger with a little 'nip and tuck'.

We work so hard to maintain our youthful appearance of our earthly physical shell, I wonder at times if we work as hard to maintain our youthful 'spiritual energy'.

With the focus on the physical earthly shell, many have asked my thoughts in regards to those loved ones who have moved on when they are in their earthly plan at youth. When a child is given an earthly plan that appears to us as completed in such a short path, does their spiritual energy remain at that age or rather mature within their spirit?

Others within the field of the paranormal have thoughts that when one moves on their spiritual energy becomes a certain age. When a child moves on, their spirit becomes mature in order for them to assist in guidance. All who have entered the other side are of one 'spiritual age'.

I feel that when our unique spiritual energy is created, it is created within a unique physical shell. Unfortunately no matter how hard we try to maintain our youthful appearance, our physical bodies are created to 'age with the time'. Upon completing ones earthly plan, the spirit created within moves on and leaves the temple of the physical body to lay to rest.
Ashes to ashes –dust to dust.

I feel we cannot associate the 'age of the spirit' with the 'age of the physical shell' simply due to one is unique to the other. For example if a loved one suddenly completes his or her earthly plan at the age of six years, does the spiritual energy remain at six years? What we are associating in this question is the spiritual energy with the earthly physical body. There cannot be a comparison in my view, as the physical shell ages and the spirit remains ageless.

Many years have gone by for the loved ones of the six year old. To validate his/her presence, how best would it be for the spirit to appear? Would the parents know it is their child if he/she appears as an adult, or would they know their child as they were when 'they moved on'? As an adult energy, the parents may run screaming thinking they are 'haunted'!

My thoughts are that the spiritual energy of a child has many choices simply due to no longer being confined to the age of the physical shell. They may remain in the 'age of when they moved on' so that their loved ones will know when acknowledged. The spirit may 'grow up' with a brother or sister still in their earthly plan so as to be 'a loving and guiding brother or sister'. Or they may simply 'age' as their loved ones will feel that the child has aged through the years since moving on.

Simply said, I feel a child who has moved on will 'be what it is to be' for their loved ones to know that life is everlasting.

Life is an everlasting gift – no nip, no tuck, no wrinkles.

Stepping Stone – Improve your spirit within daily; your life is everlasting

Stepping Stones – Life Everlasting

This cannot be all there is. Life does not end in a slow riding hearse. Fear of the unknowing.

The following pages touches on the thoughts of 'life-after' and what may be. Questions of spiritual energies, and the faith we share within.

Stepping Stones

Why Don't They Call?

Why don't they call?

The other day while watching television a popular commercial from a cellular phone service came on the screen asking the question *"Can you Hear Me Now?"*

While watching the guy walking from one area to another, I started thinking how this scenario relates to another thought. When a loved one moves on, in our state of sadness and grief nothing would comfort us more than receiving a 'call' (or a sign) from our loved one. When we do not receive any signal, we quickly walk from one area to another looking for that sign of faith and hope. In other words, we so deeply want acknowledgment that they are still with us that we tend to ignore the true blessings that we receive. These include the fond and happy memories during their earth's plan, the love that they shared, and the communication within. By opening your heart and mind, you may start noticing actual 'sense of their presence'. These may include a picture or item that reminds you of them that you suddenly find, or perhaps a song you hear, or just the feeling that they are near.

I personally feel that these are not by coincidence, but rather a validation to you that their love is still there...and also your loved one.

So stop walking around asking 'Can You Hear Me Now?' Your communication of love within your heart is a very strong signal, and you will receive your 'call' in time.

Good.

Stepping Stone – Learn patience with your loved ones; their time frame is eternal

Stepping Stones

What Is In A Name?

I was really intrigued by this question the other day, so much so that I decided to share my thoughts with you in this article.

My abilities have brought to me many inspiring experiences, new friendships, and many questions regarding what some may call the paranormal but I would define as life-everlasting. The question was very basic yet very strong;

Do our loved ones maintain their same names when they move on?

I must admit it caught me completely off guard, I think mainly because I had never really thought about it. Throughout my life as well as today in sessions with others, I just accept what was relayed to me and never give it a second thought. But when I was asked this question, I asked guidance for answers.

I have found that when we move-on, the earthly things that are so important to us while on earth are insignificant when we move on. Earthly things such as material possessions, pain and sadness is no longer a part of life everlasting. Love, togetherness, without pain, and happiness always appears to come through. But then again, are not those the 'true treasures in life'?

A loved one's name appears to be one of those 'not important now, but will acknowledge for validation' when I relay messages. I often wonder why at times they do not just 'say the name'. It is funny actually. When I relay, it is as though they are telling me in a muffled voice. At the same time, I found that when the personal name is important to relay to the loved one, it is as clear as a bell. This is why at times I seem to guess, or give the first and second letters as I only catch a part of it and other times I relay the name without any question.

My thoughts? I feel that when we move on we know our loved ones through our pure bond of love and earthly names are not in need. They know what life everlasting truly is, and because of this I do not question how they relay their messages. They will know if their earthly name is an important validation. *They also know life is an everlasting gift and it is not what is in a name, but rather love is the name.*

Stepping Stone – How you walk in life's plan determines the steps of your position in life

Stepping Stones

Feelings From A Cemetery

I receive questions on a daily basis, and just the other night in a session I received one that I have answered with heartfelt belief. The question was
"Do you feel anything when you walk through a cemetery or a gravesite?"

As the question was asked, I had to smile as this same question was asked just the day before from someone who was worried about living near a cemetery. But the person followed up with the following statement; *"I can imagine with your abilities how it must be."*

I believe they were quite surprised of my answer, and you may be just as well.

As you know, I believe that each one of us as a spirit is created into an earthly shell (or body). As we grow in our life's plan, we learn to understand, to love, and to experience the earthly emotions on earth. We also learn from our 'choices' that we make in order to assist when we guide our loved ones upon the completion of our earth's plan. Upon completion, our earthly shell no longer has a need, as the spirit 'in an instant' leaves the earthly shell. Thus the loved one moves on, and experiences life everlasting from our creator.

So the question 'Do you feel anything when you walk through a cemetery?' for me is easy to answer. I feel that loved ones who have moved on are with their loved ones still in earth's plan to guide and to continue sharing their love.

Ask yourself this question; if you had a choice to remain in an earthly body six feet in the ground or be near with your loved ones, which choice would you take?

Have I ever felt 'messages' from a cemetery? Only when their loved ones who are still in their earth's plan is with me. For example, if you visit a resting site for your loved one and 'feel' their presence, you probably do.

They were with you before you went to the resting place; and they will be with you when you leave.

Stepping Stone – To honor in memory; to meditate in remembrance; to know they are with you in spiritual energy.

Stepping Stones

Will You Know My Name?

Several years ago a legendary singer and songwriter introduced a song that was a dedication to his young son who had suddenly moved on. The song asked the question

"Will you know my name, if I saw you in heaven?"

While listening to this song playing on the radio the other day, I begin to focus on the medley of love that the words created. The writer felt a piece of him had been stripped from his earthly plan, and he questioned the thought of life-after. Deep within, he somehow felt the value of belief and through faith knew that someday he would be with his loved one once again. Still within his earthly path, his questions were simple but profound.

"Will you know me, when I see you again?"

Many have asked the question 'Will we know each other when we move on?' One wonders if we are an 'energy of spirit' when we move on, how will we know who is who? Will my brother know my sister, or my great grandmother know her great grandson? Profound questions filled with the value of belief and faith.

I feel that we are each created with a unique spirit that is given a unique earthly plan. Along our earthly path as we grow are those who establish memories and experiences. Our most unique and valid memories are those from our loved ones. I can still recall my grandmother's twinkle in her eye and her beautiful laugh. My father and I setting together in our front yard as he shared stories of his childhood days with his father. How my mother would fill the kitchen with a song and the delicious aroma of unforgettable dinners. Memories and experiences which somehow remain embedded within me, possibly because it is not within my mind but affixed deep within my spirit.

I feel that when we move on, these loving memories remain for us to remember forever. They are a part of our earthly plan, and so were our loved ones.

Why would those who love us so much suddenly lose this gift that was given in their earthly plan, to forget those they love? I do believe that we will not have the 'titles' that we became while in earth's plan, such as mother or father. I feel that we will have the 'love' of those earthly titles when one moves on, and we will know one another from the gift of 'earthly memories that we are to remember'.

To the legendary songwriter...*he will not only know your name, he will have a welcome hug waiting for you.*

Stepping Stone – love never is left behind nor forgotten

Stepping Stones

Ageless Wonders

I was cordially invited recently to share a session with a group of five. Toward the end of the session, a loved one who had moved on acknowledged his presence. Although the little one moved on as a newborn, his energy came through as a happy and joyful four-year old. It had been four years since he had moved on. The question:

"Why do energies of loved ones come through as different ages?"

It is my belief that our earthly body is a shell created for our energy. Although the shell ages with deterioration, our energy (or spirit) remains as created. When a loved one moves on, it is not the physical shell that moves, but the energy itself. The earthly shell becomes 'dust to dust'.

So why does a loved one come through sometimes in an 'earthly physical image'? I feel to assist you in acknowledgement. For example, the little one in the session came through as he would be in a 'four year old earthly shell image'. I truly feel this was to acknowledge to his loved ones that he 'is with them, happy, and growing in faith'.

My abilities have taught me to 'not to try and question why, but to listen and to learn'. One thing that I have learned while listening...
our spirit is full of love with an ageless wonder.
What a gift.

Stepping Stone – To know from within; as it is always there in the form that you know within

Stepping Stones

Favorite Love
With An Everlasting Gift

The other day I was having a conversation with a member of my family. The topic of the discussion was how during our years of childhood we thought one of us would always seem to be the spoiled one who got away with everything, or how one would get away with everything because they were the youngest, oldest, middle, etc. I have to admit even today my brother and sisters who I love so much still tease each other about being 'the favorite'.

So what about when a loved one moves on? Do they 'pick a favorite' to relay messages and be with? If a family is together with me in a session, why does it seem at times the loved ones 'single someone out' and may not relay messages at all to others in the family?

Although my abilities have been with me for as long as I can remember, I still learn something new everyday about the gift of life. I know that while here in earth's plan, we cannot begin to understand the wonder and awe of life everlasting when we move on. They know the answers...I just listen.

I feel that when a loved one moves on and relays messages (physical messages, sleep state messages, or other) they know that it is the right time and reason to relay the message to their loved one here in earth's plan. It may be because of a struggle or trial the loved one is going through. It could be the loved one needs special guidance at this time. Or it could be that this loved one needs a 'rebuilding of faith and hope' during this time.

But just because they single out one, does not mean they have forgotten the others that made their life a gift. When one moves on, I truly feel that the love in the energy is a thousand times more than we can even imagine, and it is relayed to their loved ones on earth's plan.

To them, each of their loved ones is a "favorite" and will be for life everlasting.

Stepping Stone – Each blessing given is to be recognized as the blessing given

Stepping Stones

The Choice

The other day while driving down a very busy street I took a wrong turn. I made a choice to turn left, but I should have turned right. I could feel the tension within my body as I quickly turned the steering wheel back toward the right street. I leaned toward the lane next to me, only to receive a friendly beep of a horn to let me know the path was unclear at the moment. I continued slowly down the street as vehicles behind me wondered if I had forgotten where I put my gas pedal. Finally, I was able to make a right turn. I continued to turn my vehicle until I was able to make it back to my starting point. This time, I made the right choice and turned down the right path of highway. I smiled as I once again felt calm within me.

At a session recently I was asked about those loved ones who have steered a wrong path in their earth's plan. *"Do those who 'took their life' on earth remain stuck somewhere between heaven and earth, or even worse?"*

Many have heard me speak about the gift of choice. I feel that each one of us is given a unique path here on earth by our creator. We also receive the gift of choice.

Although we are given guidance along our path, we have the ability to make choices. Sometimes our choice may be the wrong turn, and at times those that feel they can no longer steer back toward the right path; make the decision to end their life's plan. We are created by a power of love that we cannot fully understand. Although a loved one may have made a choice that wasn't planned in one's path, forgiveness
is another great gift we are given. In sessions, these loved ones seem to come through in a special energy. It is as though they have 'went through lessons' to learn about love and life once again.

I am not stating that all who 'stopped their path' have the choice to move on basically because of their total absence of love while in earth's plan. Those who have true love within but their earth's trials created a tension they thought was a dead end, find in life everlasting...
there is an everlasting calm.

Stepping Stone – Choices in life are guided; all you have to do is ask for the directions

Stepping Stones

Guidance Never Sleeps

My eyes shot open and I stood straight up from my otherwise peaceful sleep. As I looked around in the darkness, I felt the cold sweat on my brow. It was so real, yet so mysterious. I recalled every small detail, but knowing that if I did not write it down in a journal the details would dissolve with my returning to sleep.

Upon wakening the next morning I could not recall the dream, but fortunately I reached for the journal and reread my entry. After studying the words and asking for guidance in the message, what otherwise would seem to be a 'scary movie of the week' became a peaceful message for my path.

Dreams (or what I prefer to define as sleep-state messages) are what I feel at times to be messages of guidance. We are at our clearest of thought during sleep stage. Our thoughts are clear from the hustle and bustle of the day, able to focus without interruption.

It is a scientific fact that our physical mind does not 'fall asleep' during our period of rest. Quite the contrary, it appears to function in a more precise state. Research has recorded the REM (rapid eye movement) of one asleep, and found the REM actually accelerates during the state of a dream. The subconscious mind is simply focusing with precision and intensity during the transfer of the message. Unfortunately, our conscious mind is limited compared to our subconscious mind, and we tend to forget the message upon awakening from the rest period.

So why do I feel that dreams can at times be a 'sleep-state message'? I feel that each of us is given the ability to 'Listen' when created. But as we grow in our earth's plan, we begin to not focus due to society relaying this as 'imagination, coincidence, or just to ignore'. We then learn to block out what is given. In our period of rest, we have the ability to 'Listen' due to being in a state of focus without interference.

Loved ones guide us in loving ways that we cannot fully understand while here in earth's plan. I feel they know that by sharing their guidance through a sleep-state message, your focus is on the message itself. In a sense, sleep-state messages are similar to 'physical validations' from our loved ones.

Both are similar in that they are *messages to be of guidance and acknowledgement,* and each *are to validate our loved ones who have moved on are still with us.*

Stepping Stone – Dreams are conversations of guidance

Stepping Stones

Guidance Never Sleeps (part II)

As a child, I remember one particular dream that appeared to me many times and for several months. Each time I awoke in a cold sweat, and even running to my parent's room out of fear. The dream was a silly one now that I look back, but for a very young lad it was absolutely terrifying. In each sequence of the dream, I was consistently being chased by ten foot tall bowling pins. They each had menacing eyes and snarling teeth. No matter how fast I ran, they kept getting closer in each dream. Fortunately the dreams subsided before I was caught by the pins of terror.

Today, I now know that the dream was not to be interpreting as something bad was going to happen to me. During this time of my childhood my family moved to a brand new town. We had moved there before the beginning of a school year, and I was nervous for the thought of being a 'new kid on the block'. There is another part to this dream, which I will share with you at the end of this chapter.

If you have studied or read about dream interpretation, you know that they consist largely of symbolism. Have you ever dreamed of being stuck in an elevator or falling from the sky? As you may know this does not mean you are actually going to be spending time in a wounded elevator, or falling from an emergency exit door of an airplane. The 'symbols' may be interpreted as a situation you are currently or soon to be in. For example, a stuck elevator may be a symbol that you subconsciously feel you are stuck in your job position. You may be guided to know that there are other 'floors' or opportunities that you should pursue. The dream of falling may be a symbol that you feel your current financial or relationship is 'bringing you down to a point of endless flight downward'. You may be guided to know that you will not fail, but you simply need to 'take control' of the situation.

Pay special attention to loved ones who appear in your sleep state message. As stated in the previous chapter, our sleep state brings also a sense of acute subconscious awareness. Our loved ones who have moved on utilize this time to communicate messages, simply because we are not disoriented by the daily activity around us. We are in a relaxed state, and are focused to the message.

So why do love ones relay in symbols and not just 'tell it like it is'?

I feel that by guiding us in this way, it also allows us to think deeply of the message given. For example if you are told this article consists of 2,422 words, you would accept the statement and move on. But what if I made the statement *"this significant article has a total number of words which is a message for tomorrow";* would you count the words then begin to think of the reason behind the total number?

I feel our loved ones simply guide us, but yet give us the opportunity of choice in our earthly plan. In sleep state messages, guidance is given and we are to learn to understand.

In the next chapter, I will share with you ideas to assist you in remembering sleep-state messages.

The other part of my dream?

My last dream of the terrorizing bowling pins had someone standing next to me holding my hand. When I looked into his face and ignored the bowling pins, he smiled and said

"Grandpa is with you, and all will be ok."

Stepping Stone – How you listen determines how you interpret the message

Stepping Stones

Guidance Never Sleeps (part III)

It is a scientific fact that our earthly shells need the nightly rejuvenation of sleep. In a sense, it is a process to force us to learn the value of relaxation.

As small children, we were encouraged to apply daily 'nap-times' into our schedule so as to maintain our happy-go-lucky demeanor. Of course at times we chose to pretend that we were napping, only to find that in early evening every small obstacle transformed us into a crying terror. As we grew older, the need for naps subsided due to one's busy schedule, but we still had the need for sleep. Scientists have determined that one's earthly shell should receive 8-9 hours of sleep per twenty-four hour cycle. Of course many have a need for more, many less. Personally, I am one that requires only a few hours of sleep during the week but enjoys a full 9 hours of pure relaxation at least one day during the weekend.

In sleep state, some have the ability to fully relax in a deep sleep. These are the ones that if a train rumbled through their bedroom, they would not hear a word. Try and wake them up in the middle of their sleep, and it is like waking up a rock. There are others that are considered 'light-sleepers'. One of my parents is considered a light-sleeper. If this parent was sleeping in the bedroom with the door shut, and I tip-toed in stocking feet into the kitchen on the other side of the house, the next morning I would hear *"So what were you doing in the kitchen late last night?"* So the fact is that we all have the need for sleep, just in different states.

So what can you do to assist in remembering your sleep-state messages (dreams)?

As we have discussed, each of us are unique in our sleep-state. Some are heavy sleepers, while others are light sleepers. There are those that require many hours of sleep, while others require very few. Due to the diversity, one must adjust and train their conscious recollection based on ones sleep habits.

Study your sleep pattern. Do you sleep at different times without a set schedule? Or do you have a concrete 'time for bed' schedule. How comfortable and tranquil is the room where you gain this sleep state? When you sleep is it free from discomfort and distraction?

I feel one must relax their thoughts from the daily events before falling asleep. Ask for guidance and tranquility through your sleep state, and for assistance in recalling the messages given. Train your subconscious mind to maintain the messages given by simply relaying to you to 'remember the messages' before falling asleep. A tool that I highly recommend is a journal.

Next to my bed on the nightstand you will find my *LifesNotes Journal*. As I receive sleep-state messages, I write them down so that I may meditate later on the messages given.

By writing them down, one also can visualize the message within the symbolized words. Sleep-state messages are truly gifts in life. Unfortunately as in our daily life, we tend to convert dreams in a 'taken-for-granted' state.

Listen, you may find that sleep-state messages are guidance for your earthly path.

Stepping Stone – Dreams are windows that are opened for us by those who love us

Stepping Stones

Skeptical Learning

At a recent book- signing event, I was approached with a question that is common to me –
"Does it bother you when someone is skeptical?"
A question that matched the event, as I quickly recalled a chapter in my book *"You're Not Crazy, You Have A Ghost"* and shared my thoughts with my new friend.

If there were a line for skeptics, I would probably have been the first one in line. Throughout most of my earthly plan I struggled with the ability to "Listen", but today I understand not to struggle but rather to be thankful.

As you may know I feel that each of us was given the unique ability to "Listen" by our creator. How often have you thought you saw someone at a glimpse, and quickly surmised 'must have been my eyes playing games' A feeling to contact someone that you were thinking about and to have the person call or drop by moments later, and said 'it must have been a coincidence'.

Each of us experiences the ability to 'Listen' but because of society's upbringing, we grow in our earthly shell and disregard our gift as 'coincidence or imagination'. Skepticism is simply not to fully understand. In a previously published book, I utilize the following examples:

In 1943 man landing on the moon was a "dream that will not happen".

In 1943, cooking with microwaves meant you had "too much medication or had been drinking."

In 1943, to have the ability to send messages or capture images by way of a product called a computer was "something that was considered impossible".

Even in the greatest book ever written, skepticism is documented. Do you believe that Moses met with skepticism when he relayed that he 'spoke with God through a burning bush'? Do you think many laughed at Noah for building the ark due to the message received?

Skepticism is simply a part of earth's amazing history, but without skepticism the amazing wonders that are around us would not have been a part of life's plan.

Skepticism is a gift of choice that allows us to learn and to grow. I respect those who are skeptic, as they are utilizing their gift of choice. I have also experienced those who are skeptical are also those who are growing within; in their own unique way.

Someday when our earthly plan is complete, we will move on and know that as we experienced skepticism. *We also were learning to understand the amazing gift of life that is everlasting.*

Stepping Stone – To be skeptical relays that one is still searching for lessons to learn

Stepping Stones

Connecting Through Reincarnation?

Columbus, Ben Franklin and Abraham Lincoln utilizing the same spirit?

In a recent Session, it was requested that I share my thoughts on the subject of reincarnation or more specifically if I felt that we have 'past lives'.

"Could we have lived as another person within an earthly shell many years ago?"

Why do we feel as though we have actually lived in a particular place or setting, but yet never have physically set foot in a particular place or setting? Why do we feel as though we personally know someone that lived many years ago, yet have no connection to this person?

The definition of reincarnation is *"a rebirth of a soul in a new human body"* (Webster's Dictionary). The definition is a comparison to overhauling a motor in an automobile. It is as though the spirit is 'placed on a shelf until needed for placement within a new shell'. I have struggled with thoughts of reincarnation, partly due I guess to the abilities given. I feel we are each created as a unique spirit, and that we are given a unique life's path. Upon completion of our earthly plan, we move on to life-everlasting.

"So could we not be placed in a new body many years later and follow another earthly plan?"

The question is truly only answered by our creator and there is no doubt all things are possible through our creator. I am in wonder each day of the many blessings both small and large given to one on their life's path. From the creation and birth of a child, to the beauty of our universe is one that cannot be duplicated.

With this said, I share my thoughts regarding this subject. As stated earlier, I feel that we are each created as a unique spirit and placed within a specially created earthly shell to follow a unique earthly path. Throughout this path, we learn and grow to understand through trials, choices, and blessings.

Upon completion of our earthly plan, we move on to be with those loved ones who have moved on before us. We then continue our choices by which we can continue to guide and protect our loved ones still in earth's plan.

I tend to view it as one huge family reunion filled with joy and love. Our 'family bond' traces back hundreds of thousands of years. Have you ever traced your family tree? You may have a descendent who's earthly plan placed him as a close friend of President Lincoln during the 1800's. You might find that a family member actually assisted Mr. Franklin with many of his accomplishments, or quite possibly sailed the ocean blue to the new world with Columbus.

Now think of your own current earthly plan. I cannot count the times that I heard from my parents 'back when I was your age, I…' and proceed to share an experience that would become sound advice for me. I now catch myself repeating this statement with my own children, as they ask for advice.

Could it be when you feel you have been in a particular place or setting that a loved one who has moved on is simply relaying to you 'been there, done that'? The loved one may be relaying guidance to you with a 'back when I was your age in my earthly plan, I...'

My thoughts are my own of course and I may find that our creator allows us to be in spirit along different paths. I somehow cannot replace my thoughts that if everyone connected to me in family sat down for dinner the table would never have and end, and the love and guidance would fill the room.

So great-great-great-great-great Uncle President Rutherford Hayes; *please pass the green beans and tell me more about when you were my age.*

Stepping Stone – A created spirit will always be a unique spirit; no matter where it may be

Stepping Stones

The Big Bang Existence

The philosophical makeup of a created person is a mystery in itself. We are each created with a unique spirit and a unique earthly body. No two are alike, even those created in a 'twin-like' manner are different in perspective.

Would it not be a boring path if each of us were the same in thought and appearance?

This brings to me a question that came into conversation in a recent Session. The question was short and to the point. The subject was a belief in our creator and the existence of our creator. It came from one who does not believe there 'is a God'. The person was very polite in his question, even to a point of total respect.

"Rick, do you believe in God and what do you say to those who do not believe in God?"

I did not pause for to find an answer, but rather to allow others in the Session to silently answer within them.

In the dictionary they have placed a title to one whom does not believe there is an existence of God, an atheist. This word simply means a *non-believer, a doubter, or agnostic.* They are those who have a philosophy that unless factual and concrete evidence can be established, then a thought of an existence of a creator cannot be.

There are those who believe that ones who believe in a creator are grasping for the hope of a place better than their current surroundings, and live by the faith that life has a unique reason.

I have written articles and answered questions regarding skepticism. I feel that each of us is created to 'choose' our thought path and earthly plan. Again if we were created each the same as the other, think how life would be. Inventions that were created may not have been in existence, poetry never written, and medical marvels never created. So to believe in a non-existence of a creator is a choice, but I feel one who does not believe simply is saying 'show me facts'.

As one with an ability that was given, I am asked if I believe in a creator or God. This question is asked due to society's judgment that one who 'does these things' does not believe in God.

Not only do I know that my creator is in existence, but my creator also guides me with more love than one can ever imagine. Within the words of the greatest book ever written it is said that one died because he listened to a medium first and God second. He lost everything simply due to following one's words over our creator's guidance.

Each day I ask for my creator's guidance to lead me on the path given.

Where can we find the 'factual-concrete" evidence? A more important question is where you can NOT find factual-concrete evidence. The beauty of the heavens and the earth, the creation of a birth, life and life-everlasting. Of course the responding answer is 'The Big Bang Theory' or the 'Theory of Evolution'.

I guess my answer would be...

"So who created the Big Bang and Evolution?"

Stepping Stone – Special creations begin with a special creator; each and every time

Stepping Stones

An Unfinished Masterpiece

What would the painting 'Mona Lisa' be without her smile, or Shakespeare's "Romeo & Juliet" without a complete ending?

The famous painting would still represent an artistic genius with brushstrokes of uniqueness. Although we may have never known the outcome of the most famous romantic play written, we could still read the words from a gifted romantic. Still, if the masterpiece and the famous play would not have been completed, would we not have missed out on a very unique gift?

Now consider the most famous masterpiece ever created and if before the creator's final chapter was completed, there was a choice from another to 'make the play incomplete'. What would those who admire and love this unique gift have missed? Considerations even more important, what gifts would the creation have experienced?

Life is the single most unique masterpiece ever created. Each of us is uniquely painted with the brushstrokes of abundant love. We have been given a great play of an earthly plan written with the words of our creator's love for us. As a life's masterpiece, we are also given the choice to maintain faith and not to lose our smile even when a chapter in our life's plan appears to be without a happy ending. Life at times can appear to be a 'box of rocks' instead of a 'box of chocolates', but I can still here those words from my loved one who always said 'the sun will still shine tomorrow'.

A question often asked is what are my thoughts of those who have made a choice to 'complete an incomplete plan' or suicide.

Do they move on or do they end?

I feel that an incomplete plan truly brings sadness to our creator. Although sadness is justifiable, our creator's love is the strongest of all. If you are a parent of a child, you may experience a sadness of disappointment from your child's decision to misbehave, but you still love that child more than yourself.

I feel those that believe in life within and life given will also have a love within that is noticed. I feel those are the ones that move on, and are 'back in school'. When one who has committed the choice on an incompletion, they once again learn why life is the masterpiece. For those that do not believe will simply no longer be given life-everlasting.

A life is a created masterpiece with the intention to complete the brushstroke of a smile and the written path of a completed plan.

We may during life run out of paint or the pen may

temporarily run out of ink, but by continuing what was created to be, we will find the smiles of our life's gifts.

Stepping Stone – Every created path has a plan that only ends when each step has been taken; in complete steps

Stepping Stones

A Lesson From Baby Joey

When I receive an invitation to speak at an event, I enjoy sharing my thoughts about life and life-after through what I define as verbal painting. Through guidance, I create a story to express my thoughts on a certain topic. An example is a verbal painting of why we receive physical validations from those who have moved on.

It is the story of Baby Joey.

Baby Joey lived with his mom and dad along with teenage brother and sister in a typical suburban home. It is a typical Monday morning except for one small error; the agenda-setting alarm clock failed to awaken the occupants within the home. Suddenly the routine schedule became a 45 minute delayed chaos. Mom, with Baby Joey in her arms, dashes downstairs to the kitchen to prepare breakfast. She places Baby Joey into his highchair and quickly grabs a bottle of milk. As she walks toward the highchair with the bottle in hand, teenage sis yells from the upstairs *"Mom, I need you NOW!"* Without delay mom places the bottle on the kitchen table and leaves the kitchen.

Baby Joey reaches for the bottle, but he is strapped in his highchair and the bottle is placed on the kitchen table. Try as he might with his tiny little hands outstretched, the bottle remained six inches from Baby Joey's grasp. Mom returns to the kitchen as Baby Joey lets out a whimper, his hands still reaching for nothing but air. As she stands at the counter with her eyes focused on the awaiting toast from the toaster, little Baby Joey wonders why she does not acknowledge him.

As brother and sister enter the kitchen, again Baby Joey expresses his message with a louder cry. Unfortunately brother and sister snag their lunch sacks and rush out the door. As a tear begins to well in his eyes and his hand still attempting to reach the plastic container of a milky liquid, Baby Joey's dad arrives into the kitchen in a whirlwind of necktie and briefcase. Again Baby Joey cries out, but once again mom and dad are focused on the fact that their daily routine is in a chaotic delay.

Wait, does mom finally acknowledge Baby Joey? She is walking toward Baby Joey, but with a bowl of milk and cereal.

THIS ISN'T WHAT BABY JOEY'S MESSAGE IS! HE WANTS THE BOTTLE SETTING ON THE TABLE!

As he glances down at the bowl, Baby Joey suddenly drew a slight smile across his tear glistened cheeks. He knows now how to get their attention. Clutching the bowl with his tiny hands, Baby Joey throws the bowl as if it were shot from a powerful cannon. To add to the effect, a scream compared to a charging hawk follows. In a split second, mom runs over to her little one who by this time shares an expression of falling tears filled with anger. She takes the bottle from the table and hands it to Baby Joey as dad wipes the floor that is now showered with cereal shapes and milk.

This is all that Baby Joey wanted. He simply wanted to be acknowledged that his presence was within the room, and had a message to relay to his loved ones. What Baby Joey had to apply to reach his loved one's attention was a physical validation. His loved ones were focused on their daily routine, and because of this did not 'listen' to Baby Joey's message. Finally he had to share with them a physical validation, a flying bowl filled with milk and cereal.

A family picture that suddenly falls from the mantel. A coin suddenly appearing in the middle of a room. A misty image of a loved one at the foot of our bed while we awaken from what appeared to be a tug on our bed covers. I feel these are all examples of physical validations from our loved ones who have moved on.

We are in a daily routine while in earth's plan, focusing on the day at hand. We tend to forget to pay attention to what may be messages of guidance. Sometimes we have to receive physical validations as to achieve the communication of the message being relayed.

Stepping Stone – A bowl of cereal may actually be to receive a bottle of milk.

Stepping Stones –
Thoughts From My Journal

A journal is defines as a record of experiences, ideas, or reflections kept for private use. A place to create and document dreams, hopes, and inner belief.

I share with you on the following pages a special key to my journal that unlocks the door to many thoughts on special pieces of life.

Enjoy my words, and then begin writing your own journal of life and life-everlasting.

Stepping Stones

A Message for Virginia

I had a unique experience this past weekend. It was a typical weekend filled with scheduled Sessions, TeleSessions and special quality time with family.

As I walked down the stairs to retrieve my morning coffee, I happened to glance toward the main sofa within the living room. In the middle of the sofa lay something that shined. It was a brand new quarter.

As I reached down to pick it up I heard someone relay *"let her know of this"*. I looked down at the quarter and noticed it was tails up. Looking closer as I picked it up, I noticed it was a new quarter honoring the state of Virginia.

Later that morning, I entered the bank and noticed my dear friend not at her usual desk. I later found she was on vacation. Setting at her desk was someone I had not yet met. She smiled as I walked up to her and politely asked if she could help. As I sat down to review transactions, I ask her what her name was. She smiled and said *"Virginia"*.

I stayed for several minutes... as she had a message I was to relay from a loved one. *Life is truly a gift.*

Stepping Stone – Never underestimate the messages; in any form

Stepping Stones

Precious Particles

A grain of sand-a valuable part of the overall beauty along earth's beautiful seaside.

While relaxing on the white sands overlooking the ocean waters of teal and blue, I thought about how so important such a small creation as a grain of sand can be. The polished granule took many years to create, but yet taken for granted. Although this one tiny particle would not be missed if blown away by the wind or ocean, it is still a creation of beauty where it may lie.

As I sat in the Florida sun, I began to think how we are like a grain of sand. You are created individually, polished to be unique in your own way. Although you may at times take your individual path for granted, you are given a very unique path. Along life's path you may

be swayed by a wind of change or choice, but you are still created with the beauty of life...
no matter where you may lie.

Stepping Stone – Significant; you

Stepping Stones

Seeds of Faith

Recently, I read a short story that I had read many times.

The story is about a farmer scattering seeds along a path, and birds that came upon the path and ate some of the seeds. One of the seeds landed on the rocky earth where it quickly grew, but withered when the intense heat of the sun came upon the plant. Another seed fell into an area of thorns, but was immediately choked by the thick thorny brush. Yet another seed fell on good soil, where it produced an abundant crop many times over.

A thought to share. Each of us are created and given a unique path that includes life. In life, we have the seeds of choice. Some may scatter and wither, while other choices may create an area of thorns. This is simply a part of life's learning. I feel that loved ones who have moved on guide us with love, and assist us to know that life's gift...

is abundantly everlasting

Stepping Stone – Absence of trials in life weakens the ability to strengthen spiritually in life

Stepping Stones

Thankful Thoughts

Answers that is unknown to a sudden change in life's plan.

This is the case of yet another missing person, and the heartache that her loved ones are currently experiencing. No answers to why, how, or where.

Within the past week I have received several requests for thoughts regarding the missing person. National news brought this story into the homes across the nation, along with prayers of hope and comfort. I have asked for guidance when responding to the requests, and my prayers are with the family.

Each day on this earth's plan, a 'trial' such as the one above is experienced. I am glad to know within me that each of us has 'stepping stones', those that have moved on and love us so.
Guiding us, protecting us, through our trials while in our earth's plan.

Take a moment today to give thanks for the guidance and love that you have, as we each are given a unique gift –
stepping stones.

Stepping Stone – Start each new day with thankfulness; for each new day is a new step along ones path

Stepping Stones

Inner Strength

The weekend of Labor Day celebrated in the U.S. is synonymous with the many years of giving to Jerry's Kids. This year I was given a few minutes of opportunity to watch this charitable event which supports a cure for a disease that strikes many earthly shells across the world. The tremendous number of monetary contributions is amazing, but this is not the real miracle that exhibits during the twenty-four hours.

As I watched, I could not help but notice the amazing gifts of life that is shared by the smiles of those afflicted. Each similar in their fight for a cure, and yet each unique in their overall spirit of life. They cannot walk nor run, but yet believe in the love of life so strongly that they seem to fly. Some cannot do the simple daily routine of holding a glass of water, but yet each drink fluently from the positive fountain of life.

As they shared a film segment of a very special young man who had struggled with this disease for many years of his life, tears were shed. Yet, there he sat in his wheelchair with a bright gleam in his eye and a smile from his heart. He did not see his pain but rather he felt his unique gift deep within...his gift of life.

As I watched this young man, I gave thanks for the many blessings.

I gave thanks for life's eternal gift.

Stepping Stone – An instrument is never in need to walk along your path; if you carry the love of guidance within

Stepping Stones

Cherish

Someone ask me the other day when I ever find time to rest. I must admit my schedule appears to become more fulfilling with each new day. Then I begin thinking of how the hours of time is pursued by those looking for *'more time in their day'*, or those that wish time would *'stand still'*. How many times have you stated *"not now, I don't have the time"* or *"I wish this moment would last forever"*?

As you know my feelings are that we are given the gift of life everlasting. We are also given the gift of 'choices'. Time isn't really the issue, but rather how you 'choose' to design your life's plan.

So, do you 'stop and smell the roses' on the days that

time is not enough? Do you 'cherish each moment of your life' during those times that you wish would stand still?

You have a unique gift, the gift of "everlasting time".

Stepping Stone – If you walk in blindness; you will miss the steps uniquely created for you

Stepping Stones

Friendship

I experienced yet another amazing experience within my life's plan recently.

At a recent book signing, for each book that I added my thought and name, I received a smile of friendship within my energy. As I sat down across the table draped with books of *"You're Not Crazy, You Have A Ghost"*, I must admit I was nervous and even a bit scared. The event's attendance was many more than anticipated, and although my co-author was setting next to me along with my sister (and business manager) standing beside me, I still felt the nervousness that created a shaking within my hand that grasped the pen. As I looked down at the book, I begin to move my blue pen across the page.

Then something amazing happened. Before I wrote the first letter, I turned my eyes up to see across from me a new and dear friend. Her smile radiated the room, and her eyes were filled with friendship. Suddenly, I was relaxed and at ease.

The evening was to be a special event for the attendees, to meet the authors and to tour the home. But the special event to me wasn't this at all. The special event was the amazing moments of friendship that is given to one within his life's plan.

I gave thanks and smiled, as I began autographing the books for my friends.

Stepping Stone – Friendship; ripples that reach out with each smile that is given

Stepping Stones

Special Gifts

Tis the season. The sounds of holiday music on the radio and a chill in the air. Children counting the days and adults rushing through the stores. For this is the time we anticipate the presents wrapped in ribbons and bows.

Some will receive many with a smile, while others will receive none with a slight smile of hope for a better tomorrow. We all have received a gift of equal value. It may not be wrapped in bows and ribbons, nor of colors of the holiday season. Some will take longer to open their gift, while others will rip it open hoping and expecting more. Some will understand the true beauty, while others will wonder why they cannot understand.

It is the same gift for each of us, from one who loves us. *The gift of life, and life-everlasting.*

Stepping Stone – Life's gifts are created in different wrapping; But all have the same content; an eternal love

Stepping Stones

He is my Brother

It is truly amazing how a loved one continues their guidance when they move on.

Just a few years ago a dear family member moved on suddenly. My uncle was one that spoke very few words, but yet always had a twinkle in his eye and a smile to greet you. This side of the family has these same traits. His brothers and sisters saw each other very seldom and only greeted with a smile and a twinkle in their eye. Full of faith on the inside, but very seldom hugged each other or shared their words of love.

Something changed when my uncle moved on. Since he moved on the brothers and sisters are contacting each other often, sharing dinners together, and sharing their bond of brotherly and sisterly love. As I write this, the brothers and sisters all flew down to Florida to surprise and spend several days with their oldest brother.

Although I am not physically there to view this amazing gift, I sense memories of happiness and laughter of togetherness being experienced.

I think my Uncle is there too in spirit, with a twinkle in his eye and a smile.

Way to go Uncle D!

Stepping Stone – By walking with your loved ones in your life's path beside you; you will never leave them behind

Stepping Stones

Love in Life

Love is in the air!

Valentine's Day, a day that is placed on the calendar to commemorate the bond of love. Retailers have filled their shelves with the aroma of roses, the poetry of cards, and the enticement of chocolates wrapped in heart shaped boxes. Gifts to say *"I Love You"*.

I guess when one moves on; Valentine's Day isn't dedicated to a specific time. It seems that when I relay messages from those loved ones who have moved on, they express a love that is filled with everlasting.

I feel that we cannot fully understand the amount of love within a spirit. Maybe this is why we need a day on the calendar to be reminded. Roses, cards, and chocolates cannot measure the love our loved-ones carry within when moving on.

Of course the greatest gift of love given to us – *the gift of life-everlasting.*

Stepping Stone – Love has a very special date; everyday

Stepping Stones

Four-Leaf Clovers

"A wee bit of Irish luck"

While the green springs up during this holiday, I thought about the word luck. Often we ask 'they are so lucky' and 'I just don't have the luck I guess'. Is it really being lucky, or is it a guided path?

What may appear to be luck could actually be a lesson to learn. Even an early President of the United States is quoted as saying *"Luck comes from hard work"*.

Personally, I feel that each of us is lucky in our own way. I would say that if you truly looked at each gift that is in your life's plan; you too have a wee bit of that luck...in abundance. *It is simply called, life's gift.*

Stepping Stone – Luck to some may be lessons to learn for others

Stepping Stones

The Biggest Trial of All

Disappointments in life's plan. A trial we all learn from along our path. Although we may not recognize a disappointment as a lesson to learn, it is a lesson to learn.

During this time I reflect on one who was created that could have taken the lesson given as a disappointment. One who endured great physical pain during his final earths plan completion. One who withstood tremendous ridicule from those that this loved one loved so much. One who physically was stabbed, tortured, and whipped.

At the end, this loved one could have easily filled his heart with disappointment; instead this loved one filled his heart with love for all. A lesson learned.

Stepping Stone – If you grasp the weakest branch before you fall; expect to be disappointed

Stepping Stones

A Mother's Gift

"Wash behind those ears, dear"

I think it takes a very special creation to receive an earthly plan of a mom. She is a chef, counselor, accountant, domestic engineer; chauffer, gardener, advisor, marketing rep, therapist, doctor, dentist, and teacher just to name a few. This spirit accepts this path knowing that within all of these responsibilities lays the most important asset given to her.

The asset of a mother's love, like no other and lasting forever.

To all spirits given the name of moms, you are truly a life's gift.

Stepping Stone – Our creator selected a very special blessing to begin your life's path; the blessing of moms

Stepping Stones

A Father's Gift

Dad and I have always had this father/son bond that is unique.

For as long as I can remember since 'leaving the nest' he and I talk at least once per week, no matter how busy our schedule is. He has this unique ability to let you know he is laughing during a phone conversation, even though you cannot hear or see his laughter. I just know he is smiling and laughing. He never verbally says 'I love you', but we both know it is there.
It will always be there, forever.

Happy Fathers Day to all the unique spirits called 'Dads'.

Stepping Stone – A father's guidance should be guided by a father to all; our creator

Stepping Stones

Taking Steps

I cannot start my morning without a cup of coffee. It has been that way for as long as I can remember. I wake up each morning; give thanks for my day, and walk downstairs to pour the 'wake up for the day' cup of black liquid. I feel if I do not have a cup of coffee in the morning; my physical shell will begin to tell me that it is too groggy to move.

Coffee- It is one of my earthly crutches.

We each have an earthly crutch of some kind. It is all a part of our lessons in learning about life. The key is to ask if the earthly crutch is that important in our life. As I sip my coffee, I begin to think that when my earthly plan is complete, the cup of java will not be as important. What will be important is each moment I am given. The memories, the experiences, and the lessons learned.

The lesson that life is truly a gift.

My coffee tastes so much better with a smile within.

Stepping Stone – When you must lean on something don't allow it to be permanent; eventually it will weaken what you are leaning on

Stepping Stones

The Lesson Steps

Do you ever have those days that appear as if every time you take one step forward, you end up two steps back?

You think you have a solution to a situation, only to find what you thought was a reasonable answer transforms into an unreasonable mess. You could look at the experience as a 'dark day in life's plan'.

I tend to look at it as 'lessons to learn from in earth's plan'.

If everything in our lives went according to plan, one would never truly learn. It would be as if you have a test and given all of the answers ahead of time. What would you learn?

The next time you take two steps back, take a deep breathe and say *"I now know what is ahead of me, as I have walked there before."*
Steps forward with lessons learned.

Stepping Stone – If you are going to stumble; stumble forward

Stepping Stones

Turbulent Emotions

"I am still angry, and I hold a grudge".

Ever felt this way before? Sure you have, you are simply part of this earth's plan.

Have you ever thought how this earthly emotion affects more than the person that you are angry with? Think of it as a boat at sea, with many other boats floating along side. Suddenly an angry storm erupts the sea waters into a frenzy. Is the one boat affected or all the boats that share the waters?

The next time your boat is angry with another boat, don't forget how the storm will affect those around you.

Stepping Stone – Anger clouds many things; including the sun of understanding

Stepping Stones

Why Me?

Why?

Many are asking the question why we experience trials as we do in our life's plan.

All know about the recent trial of devastation experienced by our friends and family in our southern states. An experience that will remain embedded in each memory for an everlasting lifetime.

Why do we experience such trials?

We all wish these types of trials would never happen. Somehow, we learn so much from trials. As in this experience, all are coming together giving through faith and love. We learn what life is truly about, and bring us closer to our realization the blessings that we tend to take for granted.

Our thoughts and prayers go out with faith and hope, as life is truly a gift.

Stepping Stone – Trials in life are like chalkboards; it can be erased once we understand the lesson learned.

Stepping Stones

Hidden Friendships

Sometimes what may appear as an empty shell actually may be the opportunity to fill with new friendship. In the past two weeks I have been a part of such an experience.

When we arrived at the Waverly for a convention, the amazing structure normally remains only with the memories of those who have moved on.

In a recent LifesGift seminar, the meeting room before the event was eerily quiet. But in both places, the empty shells soon filled with the laughter and visible enjoyment of friendship.

Maybe if inside your own shell you feel emptiness, why not fill it with the joy of friendship.

It just may be a life experience

Stepping Stone – Sow the seeds of friendship; you will
be amazed with the beauty of
your garden

Stepping Stones

Treats

Trick or Treat!

   As I was listening to my little nephew the other day telling me with a twinkle in his eye about his Halloween costume, I could not help but recall the days of my childhood. How we would create a costume to become the cartoon character that we admired each Saturday morning. Dad and Mom walking us to the door and with the paper sack opened wide, waiting for the friend behind the door to fill our bags with chocolate and bubble gum. Going home that evening, spreading the candy on the floor in little piles and filling our little bellies until we could not eat anymore.

During the season of spooky images think about the 'bags of sweets' in your life, and like my nephew – get that gleam in your eye.

Stepping Stone – Maintain the spirit of a child within you; the little things along your path will then become significant

Stepping Stones

Soul Food

Before you stuff yourselves with the feast of the holiday, fill your inner spirit with thoughts of your blessings given to you along your earthly path.

Start off with a slice of bread - your bread of life. Follow up with the main course - your family that surrounds you, still on earth and those who have moved on. Finish off with a delicious dessert - All that you have and all that has been given to you.

Don't forget to wipe your chin with a smile.

Stepping Stone – By truly understanding one's blessings; will fulfill the spirit within

Stepping Stones
Step by Step

About Life's Path

Page 4
Life-Trials - *Understand that with each trial in life there is a lesson of learning and a stepping stone of guidance.*

Page 11
Family-Your Importance - *A family is created with a reason of importance, and it begins with you.*

Page 15
Life-Daily Routines - *Never take for granted what is to become an everlasting memory.*

Page 36
Life-Judging Others - *Before you judge a book, learn to first read the energy within.*

Page 43
Life- Path in Life - *a clearer path in life begins with clearing the path in life*

Page 53
Family- Your Position - *You have a purpose for the generations that are yet created.*

Page 64
Life-Loved One Moving On - *Begin with a positive outlook, continue with a persistent outlook of being blessed.*

Page 166
Life - *Significant; you*

Page 168
Life - *Absence of trials in life weakens the ability to strengthen spiritually in life*

Page 170
Life - *Start each new day with thankfulness; for each new day is a new step along ones path*

Page 174
Life - *If you walk in blindness; you will miss the steps uniquely created for you*

Page 176
Life - *Friendship; ripples that reach out with each smile that is given*

Page 177
Life - *Life's gifts are created in different wrapping; But all have the same content; an eternal love*

Page 182
Life - *Love has a very special date; everyday*

Page 183
Life - *Luck to some may be lessons to learn for others*

Page 185
Life - *If you grasp the weakest branch before you fall; expect to be disappointed*

Page 187
Life - *Our creator selected a very special blessing to begin your life's path; the blessing of moms*

Page 189
Life - *A father's guidance should be guided by a father to all; our creator*

Page 192
Life - *When you must lean on something don't allow it to be permanent; eventually it will weaken what you are leaning on*

Page 194
Life - *If you are going to stumble; stumble forward*

Page 195
Life - *Anger clouds many things; including the sun of understanding*

Page 198
Life - *Trials in life are like chalkboards; it can be erased once we understand the lesson learned.*

Page 199
Life - *Sow the seeds of friendship; you will be amazed with the beauty of your garden*

Page 202
Maintain the spirit of a child within you; the little things along your path will then become significant

Page 203
Life - *By truly understanding one's blessings; will fulfill the spirit within*

About Life After

Page 7
Life Everlasting- Love One Moving On - *You are created with a gift of knowing. Just listen to what you feel.*

Page 24
Life Everlasting-Guidance & Protection - *We protect and guide through life, and receive protection and guidance throughout life*

Page 58
Life Everlasting-Loved One Moving On/Child – *The energy of spirit is created before the first breath of life is given*

Page 61
Life Everlasting-Path in Life - *To anticipate with patience, is shared through each one loved.*

Page 67
Life Everlasting - *Sadness is a true emotion given for a reason, to expand the happiness that is yet to come.*

Page 80
Life Everlasting - *One is never too old or too young to learn – and to Listen.*

Page 104
Life Everlasting - *Learn patience with your loved ones; their time frame is eternal*

Page 154
Life Everlasting - *Every created path has a plan that only ends when each step has been taken; in complete steps*

Page 180
Life Everlasting - *By walking with your loved ones in your life's path beside you; you will never leave them behind*

About Life's Physical Abilities

Page 19
Life-Searching for Answers - *What you think is the right path of decision may be the wrong path for guidance.*

Page 27
Life-Physical Abilities - *What we are given within will overcome what we are given without.*

Page 31
Life-Abilities - *Even the simple things creates smiles in life.*

Page 48
Life-Physical Abilities - *Do not lose sight of what is cherished- life*

Page 71
Life Everlasting - *Pain experienced within our physical shell is left behind – with our physical shell*

Page 172
Life - *An instrument is never in need to walk along your path; if you carry the love of guidance within*

About the Haunted Life

Page 75
Life Everlasting - *What may be a structure for some, are eternal memories for others.*

Page 84
Life Everlasting - *A validation of presence is an acknowledgement of guidance.*

Page 87
Life Everlasting - *Memories are captured within – the spirit captures the love to share eternally.*

Page 92
Life Everlasting - *The spirit of evil is created on earth – and remains on earth*

Page 96
Life Everlasting - *Spiritual energies are tour guides for understanding lessons learned*

Page 110
Life Everlasting - *To honor in memory; to meditate in remembrance; to know they are with you in spiritual energy.*

Page 159
Life Everlasting - *A bowl of cereal may actually be to receive a bottle of milk.*

Page 164
Life Everlasting - *Never underestimate the messages; in any form*

About Spiritual Energies in Life

Page 39
Life-Guidance & Protection - *The hills of trials we sometimes endure are not quite as steep when you are carried with guidance and faith*

Page 100
Life Everlasting - *Improve your spirit within daily; your life is everlasting*

Page 107
Life Everlasting - *How you walk in life's plan determines the steps of your position in life*

Page 115
Life Everlasting - *love never is left behind nor forgotten*

Page 118
Life Everlasting - *To know from within; as it is always there in the form that you know within*

Page 121
Life Everlasting - *Each blessing given is to be recognized as the blessing given*

Page 125
Life Everlasting - *Choices in life are guided; all you have to do is ask for the directions*

Page 129
Life Everlasting - *Dreams are conversations of guidance*

Page 134
Life Everlasting - *How you listen determines how you interpret the message*

Page 138
Life Everlasting - *Dreams are windows that are opened for us by those who love us*

About the Skeptical Life
Page 141
Life - *To be skeptical relays that one is still searching for lessons to learn*

About the Reincarnation of Life
Page 146
Life Everlasting - *A created spirit will always be a unique spirit; no matter where it may be*
Page 150
Life Everlasting - *Special creations begin with a special creator; each and every time*

If you enjoyed Stepping Stones: Thoughts Along Life's Path please leave a review on Amazon

About The Author – Rick Hayes

As a Paranormal Communications Consultant, Rick consults on a daily basis with those that have questions regarding life and one's path on earth. Since bringing his consulting abilities to the public, Rick has assisted thousands in understanding that life is a gift of everlasting.

At an early age Rick realized that he had been given the unique ability to relay messages from those who have moved on. Born and raised in a Christian environment, his belief that our creator has given us the gift of everlasting life through faith has remained throughout his own earthly plan.

Rick is the founder of LifesGift, Inc. and also an author and speaker. Rick has appeared on radio, television, and live events. He also writes an online column 'Rick's LifesNotes' and articles for other publications as well.

For more Information visit us at our website

www.lifesgift.com

Other Books by Rick Hayes
A Must Read

'You're Not Crazy, You Have A Ghost'

Read the book written by Rick Hayes and co-author Karen Coons that shares the experiences from a 'ghostly' home, and the answers of understanding from a Paranormal Communications Consultant.

Available at
www.lifesgift.com
www.amazon.com

Also From Stellium Books
Best Seller in Supernatural on Amazon

<u>Amazing Paranormal Encounters Volume 1</u>

If you enjoy books about ghosts and hauntings, especially truly creepy books of real experiences, this is an awesome read that has twelve chapters of amazing accounts by twelve different people. A collection of real stories about ghosts and hauntings by notable paranormal personalities.

www.ingramcontent.com/pod-product-compliance
Lightning Source LLC
Chambersburg PA
CBHW070656100426
42735CB00039B/2168